# Book Description

Does he act mean, rebellious, and undisciplined? Are you getting one-word replies back from him? Do you wish you were closer to him, like old times?

Teenage boys have minds of their own. They also have mood swings; one day he'll be talkative and helpful, and the next he'll be gloomy, secretive, and shallow.

With so many hormonal changes happening inside them, they are as confused as you are. Parents have it a little rough, because they've been used to looking after their boy... and then suddenly, he doesn't need them anymore. Without proper knowledge on how to raise this almost-stranger living in your house, who's been eating like a monster and staying locked in his room all day, it can be hard to know how to raise them into being responsible, empathetic, respectful, and disciplined adults.

In this brief, groundbreaking guide, Frank Dixon discusses the seven parental skills he finds most effective in raising, understanding, and communicating with teenage boys. With his profound knowledge and expertise in the area, he offers readers a glimpse into his methodologies in facilitating parents' raising of confident and intelligent boys.

Readers will find that his seven vital parenting skills are backed by science, and that they make a remarkable difference in the lives of both parents and teenagers.

With both wit and passion, Frank spills the beans on what works and what doesn't while guiding parents on how to learn each skill, and later apply it to their own boys.

Trust Frank, and you will not regret it!

# Effective Communication for Divorced Families

## 7 Ways to Communicate Effectively in a Divorced or Separated Family

Frank Dixon

professional advice. The content within this book has been derived from various sources. Please consult a licensed professional before attempting any techniques outlined in this book.

By reading this document, the reader agrees that under no circumstances is the author responsible for any losses, direct or indirect, that are incurred as a result of the use of the information contained within this document, including, but not limited to, errors, omissions, or inaccuracies.

Before we begin, I have something special waiting for you. An action-packed 1 page printout with a few quick & easy tips taken from this book that you can start using today to become a better parent right now!

It's my gift to you, free of cost. Think of it as my way of saying thank you to you for purchasing this book.

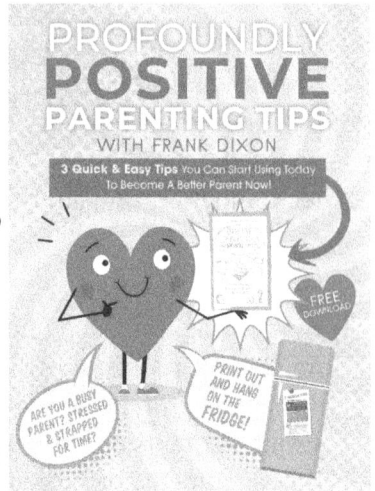

**Claim your download of Profoundly Positive Parenting with Frank Dixon by scanning the QR code below and join my mailing list.**

Sign up below to grab your free copy, print it out and hang it on the fridge!

**Sign Up By Scanning The QR Code With Your Phone's Camera To Be Redirected To A Page To Enter Your Email And Receive INSTANT Access To Your Download**

# Table of Contents

# Introduction

Parents getting divorced or separated are often worried about how it's going to change and affect the lives of their kids. They are worried that it will distort the image of healthy relationships in front of the kids, and that they will never grow up to experience the love, care, respect, and compassion partners should have for one another. Deciding to get a divorce—or separate—on mutual terms is a tough decision to make. Unlike in other cases where the divorce is unconsented and one or both partners have been accused of cheating, adultery, or abuse, consented divorce in or outside court is a hard decision to take for both partners. They have to talk about custody handlings, how the kids will blend in both families separately, and what will happen when one parent decides to date or remarry. These issues often turn both partners bitter towards one another and they try to turn the kids against their ex as a result of untreated, heated emotions. They want to blame the other parent for not making enough effort or being unkind towards the family unit and thus construct reasons as to why children should form hatred towards them too.

However, this shouldn't be the case.

If you are reading this book, chances are that divorce has already touched your life and affected you and your kids. You are here because you are looking for ways to deal with the trauma, heal, and help your kids cope with the change. You want to raise them as healthy and happy adults, and would further like to set an example for them.

The first step is to keep them in the loop about everything that's been going on. No matter what age they are, kids are sensitive and in need of all the love and care you have to give. They want to feel included and important. They want to know why their parents don't want to live together anymore, and whether it is their fault or not.

This book serves as guidance for those parents seeking ways to navigate the emotional midfield they are in. They want to initiate those tough but crucial conversations with their children and wish to do them in a healthy, constructive, and effective way. They want to be prepared to answer all the questions that their children might have for them. They want to be able to reassure the kids that they will forever be the top priority and no harm will come to them. And most importantly, they wish to reassure that things will be alright once all the dust settles down and further promise them a healthy living environment.

In this book, we will explore the theme of effective communication as well as how parents can reassure their children that a divorce doesn't dissolve the relationship between the parents. This is only possible when you can develop a strong co-parenting strategy following the divorce or separation. Like any business, a successful relationship relies on trust and openness. Since the goal is to raise a well-adjusted kid despite the divorce settlement, healthy and effective communication with the kids is the key to it.

So, let's kick this off with the psychological effects a divorce can have on your kid(s) to better understand the seriousness of the situation. Remember, just because you two can't stand each other doesn't mean that the child should have to choose between their parents. A well-functioning household requires both, a father and a mother, to ensure their proper mental and emotional upbringing.

# Chapter 1:

# Mommy and Daddy Don't

# Want to Live Together

As parents, our top priority is to provide our children with the best in-house care and love possible. We want them to be happy, healthy, and well-adjusted. We want to do everything in our power to not disappoint or hurt them. Yet, we know that a divorce is going to do just that! Most parents stay in unhappy marriages for the sake of the kids. They rarely talk to one another, fight over small issues, and are always out to get one another. What they don't realize is that this too affects the kids, and not in a positive light. Our children want to see us happy too. They might not like to see us kiss or be cheeky with one another, but such acts do assure them that their parents are happy and in love together.

So when living together doesn't remain a possibility, parents fear how it is going to affect the children. They fear their kids won't be able to take the separation well.

But in all honesty, separating from one another is better than living together miserably. If you have decided to execute a divorce, it is possible to choose a path that doesn't involve guilt, shame, anger, or any other toxic byproduct. The key to achieving this is through effective communication. However, before we get to that, in this first chapter, we are going to explore the emotional turmoil and psychological trauma that children go through and how they react to that trauma.

There are several studies (Musick & Meier, 2010) that suggest that children that grow up in two-parent households with their biological parents present a positive range of outcomes than those that grow up in single-parent families. Single parenthood has reportedly been linked with higher rates of school dropouts, juvenile delinquency, teenage pregnancy, and other negative outcomes. However, we can't reduce all that a parent does for their child to negative behaviors. A divorce or separation may be the reason that triggers it, but it certainly isn't the only one. Besides, parents can live happily separately too. They can act decent and respectful towards one another, which can build a positive and healthy environment for the child.

Speaking of some more studies, below are some that promote the idea of a two-parent household.

Having a solid and intact family affects a child's upbringing positively, as well as their future. During one study, it was revealed that children that grow up in two-parent families who have been married continuously are less likely to suffer or depict a wide range of academic, cognitive, and social-emotional problems in adulthood. (Reeves & Howard, 2013).

In another study, researchers found that children that grow up in traditional nuclear families are more likely to go to college and graduate high school than those raised by single-parent or blended families. (Ginther & Pollak, 2004).

In traditional two-parent families, children have more access to community and economic resources since parents are more available to pool their time, energy, and money on their kids. Children seem to be the central focus of those families. One study (Manning & Lamb, 2003) closely studied the link and also found out that kids growing up in intact families were less likely to exhibit behavioral problems in school and with their peers as opposed to those living with single parents.

Children living with their biological parents are twenty to thirty-five percent healthier than those living in broken homes (Dawson & Wymbs, 2016). Dawson's research also points out that family intactness also reduces the instances of out-of-wedlock births, teenage abortions, and better employment rates when the kids grow up.

In short, children living with both their parents have a stable family environment, given the parents aren't out to get one another. There is an establishment of consistent routines that helps build structure and discipline in a child's life, unlike when the parents are divorced and the children are expected to follow the rules of two different homes. They are often found complaining that their dad/mom lets them do this (like order-in food instead of eating home-cooked meals).

Kids living with happily married parents are more engaged in community activities, actively take part in academic pursuits, and are more passionate and driven about their career (Teachman & Paasch, 1994).

This suggests that living together does have benefits on the well-being of the child. They seem to receive a more stable and sound environment essential for their mental and emotional health. They also seem to be more connected with themselves and their parents, which makes room for open communication to happen. Not to mention, children also feel more loved and valued in homes where they sense happiness and compassion for one another.

However, what happens when things change between parents? What happens when they decide to part ways and leave them hanging in between? What about when children have to pick sides and follow the rules of two different homes? Or when they have to move away to another house, leave their friends behind, and enroll in a new school?

# The Psychological Effects of Divorce on Kids

Numerous studies talk about the dangers of parental separation and how it affects children. Divorce and separation are linked with a wide range of negative outcomes for the children, especially, if they are adolescents. Children living with single parents have shown to do poorly in academics than those living in healthy and complete homes. They prematurely drop out of school and have been shown to exhibit disruptive behaviors. Some studies also suggest that they are more likely to get into fights, drugs, alcohol, and stealing when they don't have strong parental figureheads guiding and disciplining them. Children who live with single parents also deal with anger and stress issues. They lash out and don't abide by the rules or stand authority. They also suffer from poor self-esteem, emotional distress, and an overall depressed mood.

Then, parental divorce also impacts their transition from adolescence to adulthood. Their perspective about strong and healthy relationships gets distorted. When they witness their parents leading miserable lives and then ultimately getting a divorce, they begin to see it as a normalized pattern. Therefore, when they enter into relationships, their low self-esteem, lack of self-assurance and trust continue to get in the way of their ability to form healthy bonds with those around them. They constantly live in the fear that they will eventually turn into their parents and have the same sad ending. To avoid this, they become clingy and dependent on their partner or spouse, which can be a little too much to handle.

Some studies suggest that children living with single parents experience poverty, risky sexual activity, educational failure, earlier marriage, non-marital birth, marital discord, and cohabitation at a higher rate than those who reside with a "complete" family unit. Since they are emotionally unstable and dealing with personal trauma, these adults don't have healthy coping mechanisms that will help them deal with the issues in all their relationships.

For most kids, divorce means losing daily contact with one parent. This, in most cases, is the father. Decreased connection and bonding greatly affect the relationship a child has with their father, reveals a paper published in 2014 (Anderson, 2014). This is especially the case with girls. Not having a male parental figure has been one of the leading causes of teen pregnancy, risky abortions, and sexual harrasment.

But that isn't all. Divorce also distorts the relationship the child has with the mother, who now has become the primary caregiver. If for any reason the child thinks that the mother is to blame, they can't create a loving bond with them. Custodial parents also report increased stress levels as they have to constantly try to connect and bond with the child(Rappaport, 2013).

Following the same theme, researchers (Rodriguez-JenKins & Marcenko, 2014) also found that after a divorce or separation, mothers are less supportive and affectionate. They may not intentionally neglect their kids, but disciplining their kids becomes less effective and inconsistent.

Besides, separation isn't the hardest part. The stressors that accompany the divorce, the uncertainty and lack of safety that develops, is what scares most kids. For them, their father or mother is their confidence pillar. Losing them is a deep loss that they don't always know how to express. Then they have to change schools, move to a new house, and live with a single parent that doesn't seem to have it all together. This can trigger many mental health problems in adolescents and teenagers. Kids may find it hard to adjust or cope with the new changes, and suffer from separation anxiety. Some kids are quick to get over it, but for others it requires months. In those months, their emotional stability remains out of whack and they lash out at the smallest of things. It is thus normal for them to experience increased anxiety, depression, and stress.

A child may also lose interest in social activities at school. They may become quiet or avoid questions about their parents as they feel isolated and unloved. They find it hard to relate with someone that isn't going through the same thing, and this isolation and lack of empathy from others can make them avoid social gatherings altogether. Children may also begin to feel insecure and wonder if they are the reason for their parent's separation. If not reassured in the right manner, they can take it to heart and feel responsible.

Some children, especially teenagers, also depict difficulty in accepting and adopting the change. This is extra crucial with the entrance of a new partner in their parent's life. New family dynamics can make it harder for them to adjust. They might compare the new partner with their biological parent and remain hesitant in opening up or expressing themselves. If they have to move cities and leave their friends behind on top of this, you can imagine the amount of strain they are forced to go through.

In such a case, it is quite natural for them to feel angry and irritated towards both the parents and life in general. For most kids, anger is the easiest way to negate their feelings. They don't want to feel sad, but they don't have a choice. They don't want to be frustrated, but everything just gets to them. They don't want to lash out, but there is so much anger built up inside them. When kids feel overwhelmed, they don't know how to respond constructively.

They can also feel an immense amount of guilt if they are aware of what's happening between their parents before the parents disclose it to them. They look at the two of you fighting and wonder if you two will ever love one another again or not. If the fight involves the child or is for the sake of the child, they feel responsible and guilt takes over. Guilt increases pressure on them and causes stress. Therefore, it is important that you sit down with your child, act like adults, and openly communicate the reasons for the divorce. Again, reassurance goes a long way. They need to know that they aren't what's causing the separation. This validation, consistent if necessary, will work wonders in avoiding the aforementioned destructive behaviors.

# Chapter 2:

# Telling the Kids

A key aspect of the divorce process is letting the kids know. Of course, they are going to be distraught, but this must be done. A lot of parents wait until the last minute to tell their kids that they are separating. This can make them feel excluded since they are a part of the family too. In most cases, the conversation happens when one of the partners has moved out and the court hearings are scheduled (given you take that route and don't settle outside of court).

Since the goal is to make communication effective around the topic of divorce and focus on the well-being of the children, from now onwards, we are going to divide the process into seven different parts/tips to make communicating easier for the parents.

Since it all has to begin with the hard-to-have conversation, the first step involves the basics of how to plan the crucial conversation. Essentially, how to break the news. The chapter will evaluate this in great depth.

# Etiquettes to Breaking the News

This will probably be the biggest unexpected shock your children are going to receive, especially if they thought that despite the fights, you and your partner had things under control. The least you can do to ease the impact of the shock is follow some basic etiquette while breaking the news to them. For starters, don't be quick to break the news. Sometimes, partners reconcile and decide to stay together. They decide to go for counseling and give their marriage one last chance. If any of you are unsure despite having decided to separate ways, let the idea sit with you for some time before the kids get the wind of it. You want to be sure of your decision and be on the same page. Once you tell the kids, things aren't going to change, even if you decide to get back together. They will still know of what could have been and the memory will remain etched in their hearts forever. So, act like adults and ensure that you are deciding upon the right time to tell them— not just for your sake, but ultimately theirs.

In order to ensure that this is the route you'd like to follow moving forward, you can try to stay away from one another for a couple of weeks and see how things move from there. If there is the slightest possibility that you decide to get back, the kids shouldn't have to get involved.

Once the decision has been made and you are both willing to live happily ever after (separately), create a plan on how you are going to tell the kids. This needs to be a proper and planned conversation. You must rehearse the reactions and prepare appropriate responses for the questions your children might have for you once you break the news to them.

Also, be particular about the timing of it too. You don't want to catch them when they are already sad or depressed about something. You want them mentally present, and not distracted. You want them awake and aware, not tired or sleepy. Additionally, be cautious about breaking the news around the holiday season because it will forever ruin it for them. The same applies to birthdays and other special occasions.

Third, tell them together. This is another important thing. Your child needs to hear the final decision from both of you. For a few minutes, forget who was at fault or who didn't try enough—for the sake of the kids. Be in this together because you are both parents to the child and are equally responsible for how they take in the news. At first, stick to the reasons as to why you two are no longer a perfect match. Don't play the blame game or get into an argument in front of them. Stay calm and composed and tell them that you tried your best to make things work but it is only causing more unhappiness. Tell them that you failed at making each other happy. Emphasize that this decision promises happiness for both of you, just separately. If they are a tween or teenager, chances are they are going to appreciate that honesty and also the fact that you gave your relationship a try for their sake.

Be prepared for unexpected reactions and responses with multiple children. Every child views divorce differently. An older child might seem relieved that there will be less toxicity in the house, whereas a younger child might be gutted with the idea and cry their eyes out upon hearing the news. As adults, be prepared to handle both of these situations with understanding and reassurance. Don't interrupt when your children are expressing how they feel about your decision. Let them have that moment and wait for them to say something.

After explaining the reasons for the separation and acknowledging their feelings and emotions, the next thing you need to do is talk about the outcomes and changes that will happen, given you go for joint custody. After having told them, this is the first question on a child's mind. They want to know what will happen now, how will things move forward, who will be moving out, how will the joint custody arrangements work, etc. They want to know if they will be expected to change schools, how often they will get to see the other parent, and what expectations will be set for them moving forth.

Surely, by this time, you and your partner must have figured out these arrangements. You must have also decided on-time scheduling. However, failing to provide them with concrete answers will lead to increased anxiety and uncertainty. They need some form of security, especially during such an unsettling time.

Also, remember to tell all of your kids at the same time. If they are adults and living at their places, give them a call and request them all to gather. You don't want one of them calling all the others and breaking the news. Sharing the news with them as a unit will minimize the hurt. Also, they will have a chance to be direct with you and discuss the reasons for the divorce. Not to mention, it will also save you some time with all of the repeated rehearsals and stress.

Have the conversations when the entire family is present. One sibling can help the other and serve as each other's support system. When you tell only one of them and request them to not tell their other siblings, you are burdening them with additional pressure and also, suffering alone.

Finally, be concrete and firm with your plans moving forth. If your kids are teenagers, they might want to have a say in who they want to stay with. However, this might not always work for you or your partner. For example, your husband might not be in a position to take the kids and could even require more time to attain financial stability. In this case, if you offer your kids the choice to pick a parent and they go picking the dad, you know it will not be in anyone's favor. Therefore, don't offer them the choice to pick. Instead, let them know who they will live with.

If they are young and naïve, they are probably going to be okay with whatever their parents think is best for them.

Chapter 3:

# Age-Appropriate Guide to

# Talk to the Kids

For most kids, the news of divorce will come as a great big shock, no matter how young or old they are. Therefore, you have to strategize how you are going to have that initial conversation with them. Chances are, they are never going to forget this conversation, so you have to ensure that you use the right words, show empathy, and be an active listener for them. Since you can't control the way they react, go prepared to avoid disappointing them.

In this chapter, we are going to look at how conversations with children can be held in an appropriate manner based on each respective age group. The goal is to facilitate effective communication with each child, so as to ensure that you can handle their tough questions and concerns.

## 1 to 5 year olds

Children this young rely on their parents for almost everything. Their parents are their primary caregivers and they are most attached to them. So what happens when one of them has to disappear all of a sudden, leaving the child confused and worried?

Luckily, they are too young to understand what a divorce is,so they likely won't remember the experienceEven if they are about five and think that they understand what a divorce is, they won't understand the consequences or significance of it.

So when you go to them to talk, use simple words and keep your sentences short. They just need to know which parent is going to move out, where they are going, and when they can see the parent again. They don't care about the details, and would appreciate it if you can just answer these simple questions.

However, you will have to watch out for their responses, as they are too young to handle difficult emotions alone. If they seem to act out of order, they might be having a difficult time with the transition. Show them extra support, stay communicative, and distract them in activities and hobbies that they enjoy spending time with.

### 6 to 11 year olds

When children reach this age, they have a growing ability to think and express their feelings. They have a more extensive grasp of words and are willing to talk as much as possible. They are going to school and have friends whose parents are probably going through the same thing, so chances are, they might have an idea of a divorce. However, their understanding is limited and so they don't know the complexities of it. Therefore, when you sit them down, use simple and understandable language. Be clear on the new rules and house arrangements that they will have to adjust with. If they seem emotional or angry, let them know that it is an acceptable reaction.

To ease the pain and anger, you can suggest or read to them stories revolving around divorce in children's books and show them how things will be back to normal in no time.

## 9 to 11 year olds

At nine, they are capable of talking about their feelings rather well. They may decide not to, but they do comprehend the gravity of the situation they are getting themselves into. However, they still see things in either black or white and may not be on board with the idea of separation. Additionally, they might blame themselves for it, so you have to be extra careful with how you break the news to them. If you can convince them that this will put an end to all the fights and tension in the house, they might see it as a positive thing.

At the same time, you don't want them to blame your partner or openly criticize them in front of the kids. You have to keep those opinions to yourself because kids can sense anger and sadness in you. It will also distort the perfect image of their parents in their eyes. Provide them as much stability as possible during this time and stick to some ground routines in the house to ensure things are the same.

## 12 to 14 year olds

The early teenage years are the prime time for the kids. Their body is changing, their hormones are all messed up, they are hitting puberty one after the other, and are desperately trying to make sense of all that's happening. At this point, a shocker such as a separation between the parents can be stressful. Although they must be aware of how divorces work, they would still need some reassurance from you and your partner that they won't be loved any less. Again, you can expect them to be inquisitive and interested in what's with the change and why it's happening, so stay prepared.

They might even oppose the idea altogether or exhibit anger and frustration, but that's only because they aren't yet fully equipped with the process of emotion management. They are in that phase where they are more drawn towards their peers and question parental authority. They might seem distant, their academics might take a toll, or they may try to push boundaries.

The most effective way to maneuver through this interaction is to keep communication open. Be honest and don't try to sugarcoat things. Respond to their concerns with empathy and acknowledgment. Don't allow their concerns to fester or go unattended.

## 15 to 18 year olds

The older they are, the easier it will be for you to talk to them about the decision to go your separate ways. You won't have to sugarcoat things to them and can come clean about the reasons for the divorce. They already know what it means because they have heard stories of their friend's parents getting divorced and are aware of the adjustments they will be required to make. They may have many questions for you and as an adult; it is your responsibility to answer them as openly as possible.

By this age, children are keener to talk than listen, which is why you will have to keep the lines of communication open. Again, you don't want to expect them to side with you and not your ex-spouse. If they seem quiet, unconcerned, or unmoved, it can be a sign of distress, too. Let them have some space, but don't leave them out on their own completely. Also, watch out for any risk-taking behaviors they might resort to and talk to them about it as soon as possible. You can also suggest options like going to therapy so that they can better come to terms with the news with a professional, third party.

## Adult Children

Children who have stepped into the professional world or have families of their own, look up to their parents' relationship for guidance. They look at their parents and think if they can make it, so can I. Thus, they feel confident in their relationships. This, of course, is for families that were always close-knitted and happy. So when the shocker is revealed to them, it can hit them hard. They might have trouble comprehending why their parents would decide to part ways now that they need themselves the most. They think that they are all alone, in dire need of company, and need one another's assistance more than ever. So, why now?

So many questions can run in their minds as their image of ideal companionship crashes down. If they have kids of their own, it can be hard for them to explain why grandpa and grandma will not be together during the holidays. Which in turn could lead to any grandchildren developing fears that their parent's relationship is headed for a divorce too.

Therefore, talk to your kids about why you are choosing to part ways this late in life. Let them be aware of the reasons that led to this point. At the same time, reassure them that they will forever be loved as they are still your children. Reassure them that not all relationships come to this end and that they shouldn't have to worry about undergoing the same thing with their significant other.

# Chapter 4:

# The Co-Parent isn't Crazy!

In many cases, especially when a divorce is high-profile, parents start to compete with one another for their child's attention. They try to undermine the authority of the other parent by suggesting that the divorce was their fault, how they were irresponsible, how they didn't try enough, how they were a cheater or used up all the savings without telling them etc. They try to put the blame solely on the other partner to gain sympathy from their children.

It might help them cope with the stress in the short run but as time passes and the child grows older, they will start to see the reality for themselves and learn of the truth. If they find out that it was you that made up all those lies about their parent, they are going to lose trust in you and hate you for separating them from their parent forever. In short, it will negatively impact your relationship with them in the longer run.

Despite being wrong, this is a typical behavior many marriage counselors see among parents. They try to win the blame game by making the other parent feel unworthy and wrong. If the co-parent was at fault, it makes sense to feel betrayed and hurt and try to project that out on the kids. But, this doesn't do you any good either. You may absolve yourself of guilt but know that both the parents are to blame to some extent. It will be wrong of you to want your child to pick you over the other parent, especially when you both have been given joint custody.

This comes as the third step in the process of effective communication for divorced families. Here, the communication involves avoiding playing blame games with the co-parent and expecting the kids to take sides.

# Your Child Shouldn't Have to Choose!

When you talk to your child in an insulting way about the other parent, the child starts to believe that the other parent isn't worthy of love. To them, it's like losing an important part of their lives. It can be particularly painful for them to find out when they adore the co-parent and want to stay connected with them. A child wants to do justice and love both parents equally. Telling them that their other parent is irresponsible or doesn't want them makes them feel inadequate and hurt. In many cases, doing so can put you in trouble as the court strongly suggests avoiding such topics of conversation as it undermines the authority of the other parent. The child might even decide to challenge the joint custody and live with just one parent.

As stated above, no divorce is entirely one partner's fault. Parents think that children can deal with adult reasoning and side with them based on the stories they hear from them, but this isn't always the case. Therefore, you should avoid putting them in a place where they have to side with either one of you and lose all respect for the other parent. Remember, the ultimate goal is to help the children be happy and lead a mentally and emotionally healthy life.

After a divorce and custody settlement, the child needs to see both parents being stronger than ever separately. They don't want to see them negating their prowess by robbing the other parent of self-respect. This can make the child build an emotional deficit. They might stop caring about both parents altogether because they just want the fighting and belittling to end. They may prefer to hide their emotions and spend more time alone than together. Putting this much stress on the child isn't fair.

Negative profiling the ex-spouse, plotting their demise, viewing them with a critical eye, and obsessing over who they are with and what they are doing is only going to rip you and your child of mental peace. This is the time when you have to act strong for the sake of your children. This is the time when you have to rebuild the relationship with them. This is the time when you have to work on your emotion management.

Finally, in doing so, you will only be losing precious time that you have with them when they are visiting you as it will inevitably result in bitterness and denial. Is this really how you want to spend your time with them?

# Co-Parenting Rules in Two Homes

Co-parenting usually means living with both parents separately. This means that there will be new ground rules in place. Things that one parent has allowed might not be allowed any longer, and this adjustment can be a little daunting for the child. But, this transition too, can be made smoother, provided the parents work as a team.

When a child is expected to leave a familiar place and move into a new house, even if just for the weekend, it can be troublesome to adjust. Consider this as the third step in communicating the change in the house rules.

Below are some action-oriented tips to help the child feel comfortable and open to this change.

First, if you plan to move out and buy a new place, have the child come over several times to help you with the décor and furniture buying. This will help them familiarize themselves with the new place and see it become one of their own. When they have a say in choosing the furniture and décor for their room, it can make the house seem their own. This is important for the child as they will be spending some time in it too. You can also ask them to pick a color for their room or DIY it yourself.

Next, think about all those things that your child might need to feel comfortable in the new space. There must be items that they hold dear and would like to carry with themselves all the time. Remind them to pack them every time they come for a visit so that they don't feel out of place. This could be a special pillow they like to take to sleep, a stuffed toy, or blanket, etc.

Additionally, pick out some special treats or items for them that you think will make them feel more at home. Ensure they have all the necessities within reach in the new place too.

When setting up rules, be sure to have some common ones in both houses. These will be rules that must never be broken in either house. For example, some of the rules can sound like,

1. Don't ask for permission for something the other parent has already said no to.
2. Make sure to finish up on your homework before time for dinner.
3. Sleep on time and have everything you need for school the next day, packed and ready to go.

These rules must be put up in clear sight so that the child doesn't try to take advantage and go against something the other parent said no to. This might portray the co-parent in a bad light for letting it happen and create a reason for more conflicts between them.

Let the child have a designated space in the new house. Don't expect them to sleep on the couch or with you in the room. Let them have a separate room to themselves that they can call their own. Let them have drawers, a dresser, and any additional storage to put their clothes and essentials in. If they are young, let them have a playing corner where you allow them to put their toys and crafts.

You can also suggest having duplicate items in both homes so that they can pack light every time they visit. These can include clothing, toiletries, shoes, books, etc.

Don't try to compete by buying your child fancy toys and crafts. If they are moving into a new house, they will be talking about how amazing the experience has been of decorating it from scratch with the co-parent. Stay calm and let them be happy. Don't feel jealous and try to outdo their efforts by doing more. Your child doesn't need this. They are just trying to open up with you and feel enthusiastic about the new change. Don't take that away from them to fuel your peace of mind.

Keep routines in both homes standard. Decide meal times, homework schedules, playtimes, and bedtime because kids thrive when they sense stability. If they feel that the rules in one house are harsher than the rules in the second, they are going to demand to stay with the more lenient co-parent.

Chapter 5:

# Keeping the Doors of

# Communication Open

Between children and their parents, communication should never be one-way. Divorce or no divorce, your child should feel comfortable coming to you with their problems and expressing how they make them feel. They should be able to talk to you about anything and everything without any remorse, guilt, or shame. That is the foundation of effective communication. You have to always keep the doors open and act as their friend as well as a mentor—but most importantly, as their parent.

Most parents think that authoritative or helicopter parenting is the only way to keep the kids disciplined and raise them as responsible kids. In some cases, this is true. However, children mustn't fear you. They should see you as a guide, not just someone that makes the rules in the house.

When a divorce is in motion, children want your companionship and support more than ever. They are losing an important part of their lives, and they need you to be there with them to help them cope. They want someone who would listen to them and offer them comfort in this stressful time.

# The Power of Language

What language you choose to stick with when breaking the news is equally important as the conversation itself. The reason we got into discussing the age-appropriate guide was this alone. The power of the right words, spoken in the right manner, can't be undermined. You want your child, no matter their age, to understand and assimilate the gravity of the situation. You want to encourage them to ask questions and express their emotions. You want them to vent out all those feelings of sadness and anxiety that they may experience right after they realize that they are never going to be a family again. Using the right words can ease their pain and reduce the impact of the news. The right words can reassure them that they won't be loved any less and will still have a father and a mother, just living separately.

Therefore, when planning the conversation, choose your words with intention. Don't get them jumbled up in complex ideas like court hearings, social worker meetings, or how they will have to move houses, change schools, and leave everything that was once familiar behind. That isn't what they need. They need to be held, to be comforted, and to be told that they are not the reason for it (repeatedly).

When they come to you, show willingness in providing the answers. Help them make the transition from one house to another or from two parents to one, easier. This chapter will focus on how to do that, starting from how to help them adjust to the new changes. This is step four of the process.

# How to Help Kids Make the Difficult Transition

Custody transitions can be tough on kids. They might have anticipated a divorce, given the parents fought often, but coming to terms with it and being expected to adjust to the changes, is another ballgame. In this step, we physically try to help them make the transition easier by getting on board with the other parent on how things are going to be from now on. Now that you have realized that blaming the other parent will only make you miserable and lead to being stuck, working with your partner will make things smoother for your kids.

Here are some tips and suggestions to ensure a smooth transition in two different homes in case of joint custody.

**Plan visitation arrangements**: Both of you should decide before announcing the news to the kids about the divorce on how you are going to divide quality time with the kid(s). This plan should not leave either of you feeling left out or not given much importance. Discuss this in-depth as it involves more than just switching homes. When the child lives with one parent, they will have to make sure to get them to school on time, help them with their homework, keep the child clean, and take them to any practices. Therefore, discuss if you both are up for it and then set a division of days.

**Once you have finalized the visitation and living plans, ask your children how they feel about it**: This is not giving them the choice to choose, but rather telling them how things will be. They can, of course, contribute and suggest what they think would be best for them, but be sure to have the final say. Kids are naïve and easily manipulated. They might want to go on to live with only one of you but this wouldn't be fair to either of you. However, letting them know of the decision you propose is important too so that they don't feel left out. You can make adjustments to the plan now and then based on the other parent's availability and willingness.

**Stick to normal routines as much as possible**: The last thing a child needs is contradicting parents. One of you might want to stick with a strict bedtime routine every night while the other proposes that they can sleep whenever they like. This can create feelings of despise for the parent that chooses to be stringent. Avoid doing so and have set rules for such matters. Children also feel safe when they know what is expected of them. Routine and structure in their lives is what they need the most to ensure things go back to normal again.

**Don't be that parent that tries to break ties with the extended family of their spouse**: Don't speak badly about them either. Just because things didn't work out between the two of you doesn't mean your child has to break ties with all the people they love. Besides, they aren't responsible for the divorce, so why should they be held responsible?

**Let them know they aren't alone**: One way to do so is to help your child seek other families that have broken up. They can befriend the kids and have someone to talk to about their feelings with. They can relate with one another and see that a divorce isn't the end of the world. Doing so will also alleviate sadness and anxiety about how things will work out.

**Don't put walls between the child and your ex-spouse**: Your child should have the liberty to talk to their parent whenever they want to. Encourage that so that the child doesn't feel left out. Ask about the time they spent with the other parent and show interest in the conversation. Don't try to put down your partner's actions by suggesting that they are careless or unworthy of taking care of the kids. Be supportive if you want your child to have a healthy relationship with their father/mother. Don't feel jealous because their loyalty doesn't lie with you alone.

**Share important details with the other parent**: Don't hold off important information with the other parent. For instance, if there is a PTM at school, let the parent know of it. Then, leave it to them to visit or not. Similarly, if the child isn't well, let the other parent know so that they can take precautions with their care and food.

**Respect the limits other parents set**: This goes without question that you must never undermine the authority of the other parent. For example, if the mother wants the child to have home-cooked meals because the child has digestion problems, don't go feeding the kid take-out. Similarly, if the other parent is critical about how the child dresses, don't oppose their action or put them down. This lets the child think that they can always go against the rules of their parents and try to disobey.

**Don't make the child your messenger**: If there is something you want to say to your ex, don't make the child act as the messenger. Communicate directly with the parent—and don't make the kids bait either. Also, avoid asking too personal of questions about the other spouse from your child, such as who visits the house, at what time does the parent return from work, do they drink after dinner or not, etc.

**Let caretakers and educators know of the situation**: Keeping your child's secondary caretaker in the loop about the divorce is also important. They can keep an eye for any suspicious or risk-taking activity the child is engaging themselves in and report to the parent. They can also help them by being there for them.

# Effective Ways to Listen, Analyze, and Adapt

This brings us to yet another important question, what activities can help them with the blow and make the transition easier for them during and after the divorce. Since most of the focus is on establishing open channels of communication, the more you talk to one another, the better. Below are three activities and exercises that will help you connect with your child better and offer you a chance to know what's going on in their minds.

## *Conversation Initiator Questions*

This might not come off as a game or activity but rather a practical way to engage children to be expressive about their thoughts around how they are taking this transitory phase. Despite seeming fine, children might have many fears and worries regarding the divorce. The more confidently they can speak up to you about them, the sooner they will adjust to the changes that come after.

However, some children that are young or shy may not be as communicative as you would like them to be. This is where you have to make the extra effort to help them do it and put their feelings into words. Below are some questions that you can encourage them to answer to get a better understanding of how they are taking the whole situation. You can ask these when you find them alone, preferably during a car ride, at bedtime, or during meals.

- How has the divorce changed your life?
- Do you know why people get married?
- Do you know why some people don't want to live together after that?
- Do you know what a happy family should look like?
- Can you guess the best thing that has come out of this divorce?
- Where do you think your life will take you in the next five years?
- Do you think mommy and daddy made the right decision?
- Do you want your mommy and daddy to be happy again?
- If there was one thing you could change about your situation, what would it be?

## *Create a Time Capsule*

This next activity is to stress the importance that feelings don't always last and people get over things rather quickly. During the transitory phase, your children might think that their life is over and that they will never be happy again. They may be gloomy and depressed, and it's understandable. One of the most effective ways to help them cope with the stress is to remind them that the pain will soon subside and they will feel complete again. To prove that you are right, suggest creating a time capsule by answering a few questions and then burying it for a month or a year in the backyard garden. Some of the questions you include can look like these.

- How are you feeling about the divorce between daddy and mommy?
- Do you feel extremely sad?
- Do you think they should have worked things out together?
- Do you think you will ever feel happy again? If yes, then when?

Answering such questions and then putting them in a jar and burying it will relieve some of their worries around the divorce. When the time comes to reread the responses they answered, they will be surprised how crazy hurt they were and how far they have come from there during the time.

### *Active Listening Weekly Sessions*

On weekends, when the kids are staying with you, plan active listening sessions with them. This doesn't have to be portrayed as a big event. You just need to find them alone and open up about your feelings with one another. If they are young, you can talk about your feelings using role-play games involving action figures or drawings on paper. If they are older, you can simply talk to them about the effects of divorce on you and present it in a positive light. If they notice that the divorce has offered you mental peace, they are going to start viewing it as a good thing too. Chances are, they will stop holding any grudges they had against you two. Also, when they begin to talk about how it has affected them, don't try to cut them off or suggest ways to help them cope unless they ask for it. Simply listen, acknowledge, and show empathy. Tell them that you hear them and that you are sorry for making them go through this. Show support and reassurance that they can always count on you for anything they need.

Chapter 6:

# Feelings, Feelings, Feelings

This next chapter looks closely at the various emotions and feelings children exhibit when they are told about the divorce of their parents. Emotional turmoil is a given, however, some specific reactions can damage their mental peace. When trying to communicate effectively, this becomes the fifth important step in the process—addressing and acknowledging the feelings children experience and how to help them cope with them.

By doing so, children will feel more in control of themselves and hopefully return to their normal state quicker.

## Dealing With the Emotional Turmoil

Of the many emotions, fear seems an underestimated emotion. The fear of abandonment, the fear of being unloved, the fear of losing friends, missing out on school, or having to live with a new parent, are all genuine concerns that a child can have. No child is happy with the news of the breakup because it means the collapse of their family. They have seen divorces happen in TV shows and movies, heard stories about them from their peers, but they are rarely prepared to handle the trauma until it happens to them.

Young children may fear that they will be left on their own without food and a proper place to live. They fear that the love their parents had for them will diminish or be replaced by another person. They may cry or act clingy to tell the parent that they don't know what to do.

### *Sadness*

Sadness or sorrow is another common emotional reaction. Children feel like they will never have happy family moments together. It is something that can't be expressed in words, but this sadness slowly begins to consume them. For them, a parent, no matter how they are, is irreplaceable. Children in their tweens deal with divorce the toughest. They are unable to cope with what seems to them, a never-ending pain. They mourn their co-parent's departure from their homes and daily life. They miss being around them and grieve. They miss the way they used to be, miss how events and holidays were when they were together.

They may not always have the blues but deep down, they wish that their parents would get back together. Notice how they are coping with this sadness and grief. Do they want more time alone, do they remain in their room all day, have they become less talkative, or their usual self, do you find them constantly daydreaming, or not showing interest in their studies, food, or hobbies? If yes, then know that they are trying to cope with the loss on their own.

### Anger

Anger is the most common and most easily deciphered reaction among children of all ages. Combined with grief and uncertainty, it can manifest itself in many ways. Adults may act differently than younger ones. You may catch your little one throwing more temper tantrums or being rude. As for the adults, you can notice that they are trying to remain distant or lash out over every little thing lately. If you have a boy, you might receive news of them starting fights with others, yelling in front of their peers or educators, or at you. They might also engage in self-harming behaviors like substance abuse, smoking, drinking, or rash driving, etc. As adult children understand the complexities of the breakup, they can direct the anger at their parents for being irresponsible and hold them accountable for how they feel. They may not want to see you, talk to you, or be with you for long. You can expect them to have more sleepovers with friends, coming home late, or not speaking to you for some time.

### Guilt

Guilt is yet another common reaction that is a product of the mind. Whether they like it or not, kids don't have a say in their parent's marital life. They can't decide if they should stick together or part ways. To sense some of that control, they start to feel guilty and blame themselves for what happened. They think that since they are the center of their parent's lives, they must be the reason why they don't want to live together as a couple. They start to self-reflect that if they had behaved well, acted disciplined, stopped the fights between the parents, then maybe they wouldn't have parted ways. They think that their poor grades and lack of interest in house chores are the reason why their parents don't want to stay together. Some even think that it is due to the prayer they made that their father would go away when they were angry with them.

They take up on themselves to bring them together and plan surprises and gifts for the parents. It is the guilt that makes them do all this. Now is the time to convince and reassure them that they aren't to blame.

### *Rejection*

Divorce happens between the parents, not the kids. Yet, many children think that their parents have rejected each other and also them. They fear that one day, their parents will ditch on them the same way they ditched their spouse and that sense of rejection can hit them hard. It makes it impossible for them to form a deeper connection with their parents. This confusion and lack of comprehension are natural. They think that they are a part of the whole deal and will eventually how to rely on their own soon.

*Anxiety*

Uncertainty can also cause children to act in weird ways. They are used to routines and structures at home and when you break the news to them about the divorce; it's like throwing everything out of the window. There are going to be new structures, new routines, and new rules. They will have to forget about all that was familiar and step into a wall of uncertainty. They think they aren't cut for that and aren't fit to adjust to the new arrangements. This unfamiliarity makes them question everything else in their life like their relationship with friends, their relatives, and even the future. To manage this, parents must take appropriate steps and encourage them to be expressive about their concerns so that they may be answered fittingly.

# Managing Anger and Anxiety

Since these two seem to be the most prevalent and worrying emotional reactions, we must address them the soonest. If left on their own, it can breed stress and affect their peace of mind. This final section lists some everyday exercises and activities to help them deal with the stress and anger that they experience and come to terms with the new transitions.

## Deep Breathing

When a child feels out of control due to anger, taking deep breaths can help calm them down. Deep breathing exercises are a great coping exercise for kids who are prone to anxiety and panic attacks. It is known to reduce the severity of anger one feels.

## Anger Management Activity

This next one's ideal for children that aren't equipped to handle big feelings. All you need is a sheet of paper and a pencil for this. Many kids get out of control and have big reactions. However, they must know that not everything is in their control and therefore, they must learn to make peace with it. After the child has cooled off, ask them to trace a circle on the paper using the pencil. Ask them to write inside the circle things they could have controlled about a certain situation. On the outside, let them mention the ones that weren't in their control. Tell them that we can only control or influence the things that are in our control and should let go of the ones that aren't. There is no point getting angry over them. This analysis will hopefully help them build a better perspective and stop with all the temper tantrums.

## DIY Stress Balls

Some kids have a hard time dealing with stress. They would bite their nails, stomp their feet, throw their hands in the air, or pace back and forth around the room. Create a stress ball using a balloon and a jar of play dough. Cut the play dough into small pieces and put it inside the balloon. Give it to them to hold on to when they feel stressed as it will help them calm down.

## *Emotion Charades*

This is for children who don't know how to label what they are experiencing. On small pieces of paper, write different emotions/feelings and then ask your child to act them out. You both can take turns and play the game. This will help your children identify different emotions and also give them a name.

# Chapter 7:

# Moving On

Letting go doesn't stop with the acknowledgment and acceptance of your feelings. It involves another important aspect—i.e. moving on. Understandably, getting back your old life after a divorce is hard. You spent so many years with your partner and surely had the best of times. If five years ago someone would have said that you two would get divorced, you would have laughed it off. Now that you have settled for one, you may have a difficult time imagining a life without your partner. There are so many memories that you just can't forget about. And then, now that you have to do everything by yourself, you are starting to realize that it's something you had underestimated. Financial issues are creeping, co-parenting, packing, and unpacking with the kids to drop and pick them up from their co-parent's house, and the emotional roller coaster is all a bit too much.

But as you move past this and gain hold of yourself, as you slowly start to feel less exhausted, both mentally and physically, you need to work on yourself.

You need to learn to move on and forget about what happened. You need to be back to your cheery self that you missed being so much. You need to embrace the new challenges and new opportunities as they come towards you. How you act around your kids, especially the kind of conversations you have with them, is going to determine how the relationship will be from now onwards. If they see you shedding tears all day, staying quiet, or in your room reminiscing over your past, they are going to feel guilty for not being able to make you happy. The sadness and depression is further going to rub off on them too, and this is the last thing you want.

Therefore, the sixth step involves moving on and letting go of any bitterness, resentment, or anger that you hold for your ex-spouse.

Resentment and bitterness are ugly emotional reactions. They tend to turn you into an unreasonable, angry, and unkind person. The hurt turns into hatred for your partner and that bitterness within you starts to affect the lives of others around you too. This can be dangerous as once you get the taste of it and realize how soothing it feels to just vent out and be angry, it will become impossible to recover from. Bitterness and resentment make others around you feel uncomfortable. They feel unloved, always yelled at, and unvalued. Resentment also affects your focus and attentiveness levels, as your mind remains wrapped around negative thoughts all day. This bitterness is what keeps you from moving forward and embracing your new reality. It's like you become a prisoner of your past and your mind. You don't deserve this, and neither do your kids.

The more you continue to focus on the past, the harder it will get to plan and strategize how you are going to act as a calm and collected parent. Your children need things to get back as they used to be as soon as possible. They need a responsible and authoritative adult in their lives who would tell them what to do next.

So ask yourself this: do you want to remain unhappy and unfit for the rest of your life? Do you want your kids to stop looking up to you as a role model? Do you want them to avoid spending time with you because you are so all-over-the-place all the time? Do you want to carry this pain and bitterness with you everywhere you go?

Because if you don't, now is the time to knock it off. We are not suggesting that it will be easy but it has to happen. You have to let go of the resentment you feel towards your partner for the sake of your children. You have to stop letting your ex continue to hurt you.

# Letting Past Resentment go… For the Kids

Here's how you are going to do it. You are going to take a piece of paper and start writing. What makes you bitter? What is it that you want to forget about your ex the most? How do you plan on moving forward? How are you going to prepare yourself to see them again over and over when they come to pick or drop the kids home? How are you going to get over them?

Starting with the first question, you might answer, "I feel bitter because I can't believe that my ex-partner is already moving on with their life with their new partner."

In the same context, answer the next three to five questions you have listed down and see where it takes you. By the time you are done, you should know where you stand and where you need to go from there. Next, reframe the bitterness and stop looking at it in a negative light. Point out the benefits of the divorce and start viewing the separation as a blessing in disguise.

Following that, you need to know your triggers and avoid them. For instance, if you are trying to rebuild yourself, you might want to put away photo albums or wedding tapes for a while. You might also want to skip going to places where you often went with your ex-spouse and distract yourself elsewhere so that you don't have to deal with the recurring sadness again and again. Remember, most of the gloomy feelings will find you when you are either hungry, alone, angry, or tired. So you need to be extra careful and just find something else to do than be alone and think about your past.

Vent out your feelings. Don't suppress them. The less burdened you are, the better you will feel. If you are having trouble dealing with the divorce on your own, seek support from friends and family. If you think you can send the kids for some time to live off with a parent or sibling until you get a hold of yourself, do that. If you think joining a support group will help, go out and join one. Get busy, pick a hobby, start afresh, get back to work, and hang out with like-minded people more.

Finally, practice forgiveness. Some people are never able to forget their past or the person that they shared it with. This can be troublesome, given the fact that you need to be present for your kids more than ever now. Use meditation or deep breathing exercises to let go of negative thoughts from your mind and in their place, welcome positivity. Hang out with people who make you forget about all your worries, more. Make time for the things you love doing and appreciate what you have in your life. Holding a grudge against someone that seems to have moved on or forgotten about you won't get you anywhere.

## Reassuring Love and Value

While you do all that, don't forget that you and the co-parent have an immense responsibility on your hands now. You two need to reassure the kids that your love for them won't change. When parents start dating again or ask new partners to move in, the children can feel out of place. You need to remind them and prove to them with your actions that they will forever remain your top priority in life.

This is the final step of the effective communication for divorced families process. It involves reassuring the kids that no matter what, you will forever hold them close, love them unconditionally, and pray that they grow up to have some of the most amazing, healthy, and beautiful relationships with their partner/spouse and children.

Tell them that although things will change, your love for them won't. Furthermore, if you sense that they have been blaming themselves for the split, sit down with them and clear things with them. Tell them that the decision to part ways was yours and had nothing to do with you. Tell them that it was mutual and both of you wanted the best for them. Say that you wanted them to have a healthy and prospering environment to grow up in and it wasn't possible while you two lived under the same roof. If they are in their teen ages, they are probably going to understand—unlike that of more innocent minds.

Promise them that although many things will change from now on, they will eventually be for the best. Tell them that you want to make things easier for them and would appreciate it if they would help. Don't hide things from them. Being transparent about what's going on and what will happen next will keep them in the loop and make them feel included. That way, the divorce, and separation won't come off as a big shock to them.

Address and validate their emotions. Don't tell them to grow up and act their age. Encourage vulnerability and openness. They should be able to unwrap how they feel with you. They shouldn't feel excluded or uncared for. Their emotions shouldn't be disregarded. Help them by recommending strategies and activities that will help them overcome the shock sooner but in a subtle manner. Increase the number of hugs, kisses, pats on the back as a means to reassure your love for them.

# Conclusion

A divorce between parents changes the life of the children forever. Despite the fights, arguments, or disinterest between parents, children feel their parents will pull through. However, when they are made to sit down and be told the big news, a little piece of them is broken forever. However, this can be avoided, provided that the parents act as mature adults and opt for healthy and effective means of communication to break the news, set up routines, enable the kid(s) to effortlessly adjust in the new homes, and cope with their emotions and feelings in constructive ways.

The aim of this brief guide was solely this. In each chapter, we looked at how effective communication between the parents and the kids can make the blow easier for the kids. We categorized the process into seven different stages starting from breaking the news to reassuring the children that the love between them will never change.

We know you can do this. As difficult as it might be for you to deal with this personal tragedy yourself, we are positive that you will not let the kids get the worst of it. If you have come this far and made a major life decision for your sense of peace and happiness, the journey from here onwards is going to be easy. Use the strategies discussed in the book and try to be positive, happy, and communicative around the kids. Let this be known through your actions and behaviors that you are fully capable of taking care of them on your own and are doing this so that they have a healthy environment to grow in.

Thank you for giving this book a read. I hope you loved reading it as much as I enjoyed writing it. It would make me the happiest person on earth if you would take a moment to leave an honest review. All you have to do is visit the site where you purchased this book: It's that simple! The review doesn't have to be a full-fledged paragraph; a few words will do. Your few words will help others decide if this is what they should be reading as well. Thank you in advance, and best of luck with your parenting adventures. Every moment is a joyous one with a child.

# References

*7 ways to help your kids live happily in two houses.* (n.d.). OurFamilyWizard. Retrieved May 26, 2021, from https://www.ourfamilywizard.com/blog/7-ways-help-your-kids-live-happily-two-houses

Anderson, J. (2014). The impact of family structure on the health of children: Effects of divorce. *The Linacre Quarterly,* *81*(4), 378–387. https://doi.org/10.1179/0024363914z.00000000087

Atkins, S. (2021, March 22). *Kids and divorce : An age by age guide to help parents.* Sue Atkins the Parenting Coach. https://sueatkinsparentingcoach.com/2021/03/kids-and-divorce-an-age-by-age-guide-to-help-parents/

Benedek, E. P. (2005, March 4). *Children's reactions.* Divorce Magazine. https://www.divorcemag.com/articles/childrens-reactions

Bodyfelt, M. (2017, June 27). *How to kick your divorce resentment to the curb.* Psych Central.

https://psychcentral.com/blog/how-to-kick-your-divorce-resentment-to-the-curb#1

Claire, M. (2015, July 1). *Coping with divorce: An expert shares her top tips*. Marie Claire. https://www.marieclaire.co.uk/life/sex-and-relationships/coping-with-divorce-an-expert-shares-her-top-tips-66167

D'Onofrio, B., & Emery, R. (2019). Parental divorce or separation and children's mental health. *World Psychiatry*, *18*(1), 100–101. https://doi.org/10.1002/wps.20590

Dawson, A. E., & Wymbs, B. T. (2016). Validity and utility of the parent–teacher relationship scale–ii. *Journal of Psychoeducational Assessment*, *34*(8), 751–764. https://doi.org/10.1177/0734282915627027

Eaton, E. (2018, December 14). *Telling kids about divorce: 7 tips on how to break the news*. Divorce Magazine. https://www.divorcemag.com/articles/telling-kids-about-divorce

*Emotional coping and divorce*. (n.d.). MentalHelp.net. https://www.mentalhelp.net/divorce/emotional-coping/

Fattorini, S. (2016, December 20). *How the "blame game" undermines and affects separated parenting*. Stephanie Fattorini. https://sftherapylondon.com/how-the-blame-game-undermines-and-affects-separated-parenting/

Ginther, D. K., & Pollak, R. A. (2004). Family structure and children's educational outcomes: Blended families, stylized facts, and descriptive regressions. *Demography*, *41*(4), 671–696. https://doi.org/10.1353/dem.2004.0031

*Helping children cope with separation and divorce.* (n.d.). Www.caringforkids.cps.ca. https://www.caringforkids.cps.ca/handouts/mentalhealth/separation_and_divorce

*How to tell your children about divorce: An age appropriate guide.* (2018, November 27). Www.lambbrooks.com. https://www.lambbrooks.com/news/family/how-to-tell-your-children-about-divorce-an-age-appropriate-guide/

Jacobson, D. S. (1978). The impact of marital separation/divorce on children. *Journal of Divorce*, *1*(4), 341–360. https://doi.org/10.1300/j279v01n04_05

Kemp, G., Smith, M., & Segal, J. (2018, December 28). *Children and divorce.* HelpGuide.org. https://www.helpguide.org/articles/parenting-family/children-and-divorce.htm

Manning, W. D., & Lamb, K. A. (2003). Adolescent well-being in cohabiting, married, and single-parent families. *Journal of Marriage and Family*, *65*(4), 876–893. https://doi.org/10.1111/j.1741-3737.2003.00876.x

Meyer, C. (2020, June 10). *This is how to cope with a stressful divorce*. Brides. https://www.brides.com/tips-for-dealing-with-divorce-stress-1102740

Moninger, J. (n.d.). *Making a child comfortable in two homes*. Parents. Retrieved May 26, 2021, from https://www.parents.com/parenting/divorce/c oping/making-a-child-comfortable-in-two-homes/

Morin, A. (2017, May 22). *The psychological effects of divorce on children*. Verywell Family; Verywellfamily. https://www.verywellfamily.com/psychological -effects-of-divorce-on-kids-4140170

Musick, K., & Meier, A. (2010). Are both parents always better than one? Parental conflict and young adult well-being. *Social Science Research*, *39*(5), 814–830. https://doi.org/10.1016/j.ssresearch.2010.03.0 02

RAPPAPORT, S. R. (2013). Deconstructing the impact of divorce on children. *Family Law Quarterly*, *47*(3), 353–377. https://www.jstor.org/stable/24576133

Ravitz, A. (n.d.). *When should we tell our kids that we're getting a divorce?* Child Mind Institute. Retrieved May 25, 2021, from https://childmind.org/ask-an-expert-qa/when-should-we-tell-our-kids-that-were-getting-a-divorce/

Reeves, R. V., & Howard, K. (2013). The parenting gap. In *The Brookings Institution*. Centre on Children and Families. https://www.brookings.edu/wp-content/uploads/2016/06/09-parenting-gap-social-mobility-wellbeing-reeves.pdf

Rodriguez-JenKins, J., & Marcenko, M. O. (2014). Parenting stress among child welfare involved families: Differences by child placement. *Children and Youth Services Review*, *46*, 19–27. https://doi.org/10.1016/j.childyouth.2014.07.0 24

Song, R. (2020, July 3). *Anger management activities for kids*. Brave Guide. https://mybraveguide.com/2020/07/03/anger-management-activities-for-kids/#:~:text=Deep%20Breathing%3A%20Ki ds%20often%20really

*Talking to your kids about divorce: Age-Appropriate strategies.* (n.d.). Www.ourfamilywizard.com. Retrieved May 25, 2021, from https://www.ourfamilywizard.com/blog/talkin g-your-kids-about-divorce

Teachman, J. D., & Paasch, K. M. (1994). Financial impact of divorce on children and their families. *The Future of Children*, *4*(1), 63. https://doi.org/10.2307/1602478

Trussell, J. (2016, April). *Activities for helping children deal with divorce*. Extension.missouri.edu. https://extension.missouri.edu/publications/gh6602

*What are the effects of divorce on children?* (2019). Familymeans.org. https://www.familymeans.org/effects-of-divorce-on-children.html

Wolf, J. (2020, November 25). *Custody swaps becoming a nightmare for your kids? Try these tips*. Verywell Family. https://www.verywellfamily.com/make-custody-transitions-easier-on-your-kids-4123658

Young, K. (2014, December 15). *Divorce and kids: 8 ways to get them through*. Hey Sigmund. https://www.heysigmund.com/divorce-and-kids/

www.ingramcontent.com/pod-product-compliance
Lightning Source LLC
La Vergne TN
LVHW051428080426
835508LV00022B/3298